A GUIDE TO
WILDLIFE SOUNDS

Lang Elliott

NatureSound Studio

STACKPOLE
BOOKS

0 11557 03190 4

Published by
STACKPOLE BOOKS
5067 Ritter Road
Mechanicsburg, PA 17055

Printed in China

First edition

10 9 8 7 6 5 4 3 2 1

Photo credits: Stan Tekiela: cover, 6, 7, 8, 9, 10, 11, 13, 14, 15, 16, 17, 18, 19, 20, 21, 22, 23, 24, 26, 30, 33, 36, 37, 61, 62; Lang Elliott: 5, 25, 28, 39, 40, 41, 42, 43, 44, 45, 46, 47, 48, 49, 50, 51, 52, 53, 54, 55, 56, 57, 58, 59, 60, 63, 64, 65, 66, 67, 68, 69, 70, 71, 72, 73, 74, 75, 76, 77, 78, 79, 80, 81, 84, 86, 88, 89, 90, 91, 92, 93, 95, 96, 97, 98, 99, 100, 101, 102, 103, 104; Richard Day/Daybreak Imagery: 12; Maslowski Wildlife Productions: 27, 29, 38; Todd Fink/Daybreak Imagery: 31; Marie Read: 32, 35; Ron Austing: 34; Wil Hershberger: 82, 83, 85, 87, 94

Library of Congress Cataloging-in-Publication Data

Elliott, Lang.
  A guide to wildlife sounds / Lang Elliott.
      p. cm.
   ISBN 0-8117-3190-1
  1. Animal sounds—Identification. I. Title.

QL765.E455 2005
591.59'4—dc22

2004017479

Contents

Credits and Acknowledgments . . . vi

Introduction 1
A Survey of Animal Sounds 2

MAMMALS
Rodents
1. Eastern Chipmunk 5
2. Red Squirrel 6
3. Eastern Gray Squirrel 7
4. Eastern Fox Squirrel 8
5. Flying Squirrel 9
6. Woodchuck 10
7. American Beaver 11
8. Nutria 12
9. Meadow Vole 13
10. Common Muskrat 14
11. North American
Porcupine 15

Carnivores
12. Gray Wolf 16
13. Coyote 17
14. Red Fox 18
15. Gray Fox 19
16. Black Bear 20
17. Northern Raccoon 21
18. Striped Skunk 22
19. Northern River Otter 23
20. Bobcat 24

Even-toed Ungulates
21. White-tailed Deer 25
22. Moose 26

BIRDS
Nightbirds and Doves
23. Barred Owl 27
24. Mourning Dove 28
25. Great Horned Owl 29
26. Eastern Screech-Owl 30
27. Whip-poor-will 31

Hawks
28. Red-tailed Hawk 32
29. Red-shouldered Hawk . . . 33
30. Broad-winged Hawk 34

Woodpeckers
31. Northern Flicker 35
32. Pileated Woodpecker 36
33. Red-bellied Woodpecker . . 37
34. Red-headed Woodpecker . . 38
35. Downy Woodpecker 39

Common Songbirds
36. American Robin 40
37. Northern Cardinal 41
38. Baltimore Oriole 42
39. Gray Catbird 43
40. Brown Thrasher 44

41. Northern Mockingbird . . . 45

42. Black-capped Chickadee . . 46

43. Carolina Chickadee 47

44. Tufted Titmouse 48

45. White-breasted Nuthatch . . 49

46. House Wren 50

47. Carolina Wren 51

48. Blue Jay 52

49. Eastern Phoebe 53

50. Wood Thrush 54

51. Red-winged Blackbird 55

52. Common Yellowthroat 56

53. Eastern Towhee 57

54. American Goldfinch 58

55. Song Sparrow 59

56. Chipping Sparrow 60

REPTILES

Alligators

57. American Alligator 61

Vipers

58. Timber Rattlesnake 62

FROGS AND TOADS

Treefrogs and Allies

59. Spring Peeper 63

60. Western Chorus Frog 64

61. Northern Cricket Frog 65

62. Gray Treefrog 66

63. Cope's Gray Treefrog 67

64. Green Treefrog 68

True Frogs

65. Green Frog 69

66. Bullfrog 70

67. Wood Frog 71

68. Pickerel Frog 72

69. Northern Leopard Frog . . . 73

70. Southern Leopard Frog . . . 74

True Toads

71. American Toad 75

72. Fowler's Toad 76

73. Southern Toad 77

Narrowmouth Toads

74. Eastern Narrowmouth
     Toad 78

Spadefoot Toads

75. Eastern Spadefoot 79

INSECTS

Mole Crickets

76. Northern Mole Cricket . . . 80

Field Crickets

77. Fall Field Cricket 81

Ground Crickets

78. Allard's Ground Cricket . . 82

79. Tinkling Ground Cricket . . 83

80. Carolina Ground Cricket . . 84

81. Striped Ground Cricket . . . 85

Tree Crickets

82. Snowy Tree Cricket 86
83. Broad-winged
    Tree Cricket 87
84. Black-horned
    Tree Cricket 88

Meadow Katydids

85. Common Meadow
    Katydid 89
86. Handsome Meadow
    Katydid 90

Coneheaded Katydids

87. Sword-bearing Conehead . 91
88. Nebraska Conehead 92
89. Slightly Musical
    Conehead 93
90. Round-tipped Conehead .. 94

True Katydids

91. Northern True Katydid ... 95

False Katydids

92. Rattler Round-winged
    Katydid 96
93. Oblong-winged Katydid .. 97
94. Greater Angle-wing 98
95. Lesser Angle-wing 99
96. Broad-winged Bush
    Katydid 100

Cicadas

97. Scissor-Grinder Cicada .. 101
98. Swamp Cicada 102
99. Linne's Cicada 103
100. Periodical Cicada 104

Master List of CD Contents 105

Credits and Acknowledgments

A *Guide to Wildlife Sounds* was conceived and written by Lang Elliott. The audio compact disc was narrated, produced, and mastered by Lang Elliott of NatureSound Studio. This project evolved out of *Wild Sounds of the Northwoods* by Lang Elliott and Ted Mack, a compact disc and booklet originally published in 1990 by NatureSound Studio that is now out of print.

Most recordings included on the audio compact disc accompanying this guide were made by Lang Elliott and are part of his NatureSound Studio collection. Recordings obtained from other sources are indicated below. All recordings are copyrighted by the individuals or institutions listed.

Recordings obtained from individuals:
Bill Evans: Woodchuck
Carl Gerhardt: Cope's Gray Treefrog, Eastern Narrowmouth Toad, Eastern Spadefoot
Doug Von Gausig: Striped Skunk
Dan Gibson: Northern Raccoon
Wil Hershberger: Allard's Ground Cricket, Tinkling Ground Cricket, Greater Angle-wing, Lesser Angle-wing, Black-horned Tree Cricket, Common Meadow Katydid
Bernie Krause: Red Fox
Ted Mack: Common Muskrat, Coyote, American Alligator
John Neville: Black Bear

Recordings obtained from institutions:
Borror Laboratory of Bioacoustics, Ohio State University: Gray Fox, Moose, White-tailed Deer, Red-tailed Hawk
Florida Museum of Natural History, University of Florida: American Alligator
Macaulay Library, Cornell Laboratory of Ornithology: Eastern Fox Squirrel (Theodore A. Parker, III), Meadow Vole (Paul A. Schwartz & Lucy Virginia Engelhard), North American Porcupine (David S. Herr), Red Fox (Charles D. Duncan, V. V. Fulva & W. Seward, William W. H. Gunn), Gray Wolf (William W. H. Gunn)

Introduction

With joyful excitement we anticipate the coming of spring, when warm weather greets the arrival of the first migrant birds and awakens the frogs and toads from their winter slumber. The quiet of the cold months is quickly forgotten and the landscape resounds with the calls of countless wild creatures. Frogs and toads peep, cackle, snore, and trill from ditches, pools, and ponds. Birds everywhere sing and call, gracing the landscape with their marvelous avian melodies. Natural sound reigns supreme.

Then, as summer unfolds and the bird and frog music subsides, we become aware of a very different musical kingdom. Fields and meadows, hedgerows and forest suddenly erupt with a plethora of high-pitched trills, chirps, shuffles, and buzzes. Behold the concert of the crickets, katydids, and cicadas . . . not exactly beautiful in a conventional sense, but ubiquitous and emotionally moving, especially at night. How can so much sound be produced by tiny creatures that we cannot easily find or see? Beauty is in the ear of the beholder, and the more we learn about our insect musicians, the more beautiful becomes their chorus.

While the mammals seem subdued in comparison to the birds, frogs and toads, and insects, their sounds are heard during every season. Chipmunks squeak and run for cover, squirrels chatter from tree limbs, coyotes yip and howl in the distance, beavers slap their tails against the water, and deer snort and stomp their feet in the darkness of night. Mammal sounds stand out when they occur, but they are difficult to predict and usually happen suddenly, when we least expect them.

And then there are the reptiles, a quiet group overall, most drawing our attention only when we hear them move. Who has not heard lizards or snakes scampering or slithering through the leaves, or turtles splashing into the water? But let us not forget our largest native reptile, the alligator, who growls like a lion and hisses like a dragon! And what of the rattlesnake, whose high-pitched warning buzz evokes fear in an instant?

Nature's marvelous musicians deserve our attention and our study. This audio guide, which focuses on the eastern half of North America, will help you recognize and identify an impressive variety of wild sounds. Included are the utterances of one hundred creatures, including most of our commonly heard mammals, birds, reptiles, frogs and toads, and insects. As you master their identification, every journey outdoors will become a new exercise in deep listening, and you will be well on your way to becoming a true connoisseur of the amazing sounds of nature.

A key to learning and remembering natural sounds is associating images and experiences with the sounds. While this guide presents excellent examples of the sounds of a hundred species, along with descriptive text and color photos, it does not take the place of actually seeing and hearing wild animals in natural settings. We strongly encourage you to be outdoors as much as possible. Visit beautiful natural areas and make listening your focus. Track down soundmakers and fill your mind with vivid, unforgettable images and sound. Let nature itself be your most respected teacher.

A Survey of Animal Sounds

Sounds made by animals usually have a communication function. They convey mood or intent to individuals of the same species or of other species. Without going into great detail, here are the key points for each animal group.

MAMMALS

Although not as overtly noisy as the birds, frogs, and insects, our native mammals do make a variety of interesting sounds. Included in this guide are alarm calls and other sounds given in the presence of predators, sounds that are used during territorial disputes, courtship vocalizations, social calls given by family groups, begging calls of young, chewing and snorting sounds that occur while eating, and more. Recording mammal sounds is a challenge because many are unpredictable and not often heard. Some only occur during a brief mating season. Others happen suddenly and unexpectedly in the middle of the night. This guide contains the sounds of twenty-two species, the most comprehensive collection of eastern and central mammal sounds made available to date.

BIRDS

Bird sounds dominate our natural soundscape in spring and early summer, especially at dawn. The melodious utterances of small perching birds is called song, and is usually produced by males alone. Song has a dual function. It helps attract a mate or maintain an existing pair bond, while at the same time it helps a male defend his territory from other males of the same species by acting as a "no trespassing" sign.

Calls, as applied to birds, are broad in definition and include all utterances that cannot be classified as song. Calls have a variety of functions: there are alarm calls, flocking calls, feeding calls, contact calls, begging calls, aggressive calls, and many others. Among many non-songbirds, there are breeding calls that function much like the songs of songbirds.

Birds also make a number of non-vocal sounds. Owls snap their beaks when alarmed, woodpeckers drum on dead limbs to communicate with other woodpeckers, and doves make a twittering sound with their wings as they fly.

In this guide, we present the sounds of thirty-four birds, including a variety of nightbirds (especially owls), several of our most common hawks, a number of our native woodpeckers, and a sampler of some well-known songbirds that everyone should know. This selection of bird sounds is aimed at the beginner, and most readers should consult other works for more comprehensive coverage. *Know Your Bird Sounds, Volumes 1 and 2*, written by Lang Elliott and published by Stackpole Books, present the detailed sound repertoires of seventy-five species of common birds.

REPTILES

In general, reptiles are a quiet group. However, our native alligator is quite a vocal creature, with loud territorial bellows and various aggressive and alarm sounds, as well as distinctive calls made by the young. Most snakes are silent, although some species hiss, and all our native rattlesnakes shake the horny rattles on their tails when alarmed to produce a distinctive high-pitched buzzing sound. In this guide, we present the sounds of the alligator and one species of rattlesnake.

FROGS AND TOADS

Spring and early summer is the breeding season for frogs and toads. In most species, males gather in noisy groups in pools, ponds, and lakes. The loud sounds made by males, given mostly at night, are breeding calls that function to attract both sexes to the breeding site. Males of most species have prominent vocal pouches that they inflate while calling to add resonance and loudness to their calls. Some species have extended breeding seasons and may be heard calling over many weeks. Other commence breeding after the first spring rains, or after big storms, and may finish breeding within a matter of days. Several other calls may be heard in breeding congregations, including aggressive calls given when males interact and release calls given by males that are mistakenly mounted by other males. We present the sounds of seventeen common and widespread species in this guide. For more complete coverage of forty-two eastern and central species, refer to Lang Elliott's *The Calls of Frogs and Toads*, published by Stackpole Books.

INSECTS

The crickets, katydids, and cicadas are known for a striking variety of sounds that enliven the landscape both day and night from summer into autumn (or from spring through autumn in the far southern U.S.). These high-pitched trills, chirps, buzzes, ticks, and zips are courtship calls made by males. In crickets and katydids, the males have special "file-and-scraper" structures on their wings, and they produce their calls by rapidly vibrating one wing against the other. (Scientists refer to this as stridulation.) Cicadas have a special sound-producing organ called a tymbal that they use to produce their loud, rattling buzzes. In this guide, we present the sounds made by twenty-five commonly heard species, a good representation of the diversity of insect sounds that you are likely to encounter.

Range and Habitat: Found throughout most of the eastern United States and adjacent areas in Canada. Prefers deciduous or mixed woods rich in seeds, nuts, and berries. Commonly seen in wooded suburbs, where it searches the ground below bird feeders for seeds.

Sound: Responds to danger from ground predators with high-pitched *chip*s, repeated from a safe perch: *chip, chip, chip, chip, chip* . . . A deeper *cluck* call is given in response to aerial predators: *cluck, cluck, cluck, cluck* . . . When disturbed, chipmunks may emit a short burst of rapid *chip*s (a *chip*-trill) as they run for cover.

On the CD
Alarm *chip*s followed by alarm *cluck*s and *chip*-trills

Range and Habitat: Familiar inhabitant of coniferous and mixed forests of the northeastern states, Canada, Alaska, and the Rocky Mountain states. Feeds primarily on the seeds found within cones. Red Squirrels are aggressive and territorial.

Sound: Characteristic scolding sound consists of low-pitched sputters or *chuck*s interspersed with high, rapid *chip*s. Scolding is usually accompanied by tail flicking and foot stomping. The territorial call is a harsh, rattling chatter or *churrrrr* that is accompanied by whining or squealing when rivals are interacting.

On the CD

Typical scolding followed by territorial chatters and squeals

3. Eastern Gray Squirrel *Sciurus carolinensis*

Range and Habitat: Found throughout most of the eastern United States. Prefers mature deciduous forest, especially oak and hickory woods, where it feeds on nuts. Frequent resident of urban and suburban wood-lots, especially in the eastern states.

Sound: Most common sound is a long series of harsh squeals or squeaks, usually interspersed with excited *chuck*s. May also emit soft and plaintive squeaks or whistles, as well as a variety of other calls.

On the CD
Typical calls of a lone squirrel, then two young squirrels excitedly chattering, ending with plaintive squeals

Range and Habitat: Ranges throughout most of the eastern half of the United States but absent from much of the Northeast. Prefers open woods and parklike areas. Most numerous in the Midwest and South; distribution is spotty over the eastern portions of its range, but the species is locally common in those places where it does appear.

Sound: Call series is composed of harsh staccato squeaks interspersed with throaty chuckles. Easily confused with the calls of Gray Squirrels.

On the CD
Typical barks and chatter of
an individual

5. Flying Squirrel
Glaucomys volans (Southern Flying Squirrel)
Glaucomys sabrinus (Northern Flying Squirrel)

Range and Habitat: The Southern Flying Squirrel is found throughout most of the eastern United States, preferring mature deciduous forest habitats. The Northern Flying Squirrel is primarily a Canadian species, but ranges into coniferous and mixed forest habitats in the Northeast, down the Appalachian Mountain chain, in the upper Midwest, and in the north-western mountain states.

Sound: Most common calls are high-pitched, downslurred squeaks, short outbursts of twittering *chip*s, and soft *chuck*s.

On the CD
High-pitched squeak and chitters of several different individuals

Note: *The recordings presented here are of wild flying squirrels inhabiting mixed forest in upstate New York, where both species are found, and it is not certain which species was recorded.*

6. Woodchuck (Groundhog) *Marmota monax*

Range and Habitat: A common species found throughout most of the eastern and central United States and much of Canada. Prefers open, grassy areas such as cow pastures and meadows, but also frequents brushy woodland edges.

Sound: The most common call, usually given at the burrow entrance and probably signifying alarm, is a sudden, loud whistle followed by a soft, warbling twitter. Sometimes referred to as "Whistle Pig" because of this call.

On the CD
Alarm whistles of an individual at the entrance to its burrow

Range and Habitat: Found throughout most of North America (except in very arid areas of the Southwest), it dams up streams to create wetlands in which it nests and feeds. Mostly aquatic, but often ventures overland in search of new food sources.

Sound: Most familiar sound is the loud *ker-plash* made when alarmed individuals slap their broad tail against the surface of the water while diving. At night, one may hear beavers chewing on wood, which can be audible from several hundred feet away. Young in dens make expressive whines and moans, commonly heard during the autumn months.

On the CD
Tail splashes given in alarm, loud chewing sounds, and the calls of young in den

Range and Habitat: A South American aquatic rodent introduced to Louisiana in the 1930s for its fur. Similar in appearance to the beaver and muskrat. Escaped from captivity and is now found throughout the southern states and in scattered disjunct areas as far north as New Jersey in the East and Washington in the West. Prefers freshwater marshes, but is also found in ponds and streams.

Sound: Makes a variety of mooing sounds similar to those of domestic cows. If you think you hear cows mooing out in a marsh, think nutria!

On the CD
Mooing calls of several individuals

Range and Habitat: Found throughout most of Canada, the northern states, and southward to Georgia. A common inhabitant of fields, meadows, and grassy marshes. Lives in burrows and makes numerous tunnels or runways at ground level in dense grass.

Sound: Metallic squeaking notes, often given during social encounters or when annoyed.

On the CD
Typical alarm squeaks of
an individual

10. Common Muskrat *Ondatra zibethicus*

Range and Habitat: Found throughout most of North America. An aquatic species inhabiting marshy ponds, lakes, and streams, where it builds nests of mounded grass and reeds or burrows into banks.

Sound: Not very vocal, but makes a variety of excited squealing sounds during courtship.

On the CD
Calls given by two interacting muskrats (probably during courtship)

Range and Habitat: A forest dweller of the northeastern states, nearly all of Canada, and most of western North America, including Alaska. Readily climbs trees.

Sound: Usually silent, but capable of quite a variety of sounds. During early stages of courtship, a female may rebuff a male with expressive mewing squeals or screams. Porcupines also produce sobbing moans, and at times may be heard grunting, whining, snorting, or barking.

On the CD

Nasal squeals (possibly female rebuffing male during courtship) followed by grunting moans

12. Gray Wolf

Canis lupus

Range and Habitat: Found throughout Canada in a wide variety of habitats, from dense forest to open tundra. Once widespread in the United States, but now extirpated over most of its former range and restricted to remote northern or western mountainous areas.

Sound: Adults in packs harmonize with drawn-out, mournful howls.

On the CD
Typical howls of a family group

Range and Habitat: An extremely widespread species found across North America. Frequents a variety of habitats, from dry desert to dense forest, and even suburban areas.

Sound: Typical calls include doglike barks and howls. The howl is pitched higher than that of the Gray Wolf. Family members may sound off in unison with excited yips, howls, and squeals.

On the CD
Howls and barks of a pair followed by yips and howls of a family group

Range and Habitat: Common and widespread throughout Canada and most of the United States. Prefers habitats containing a mix of forest, meadows, and brushy areas.

Sound: Common call is a harsh doglike bark or yap, or a more extended hissing screech. Young produce excited chuckles and squeals when begging for food.

On the CD

Typical barks and squeals of three different adults followed by begging calls of a pup

Range and Habitat: Found throughout much of the United States in wooded areas, where it regularly climbs trees. Barely ranges into Canada along the southern border.

Sound: Barks like a dog when alarmed. Other calls include harsh growls and yips.

On the CD

Doglike barks of one fox followed by typical harsh calls from two others

Range and Habitat: Found in forests, swamps, and tundra throughout most of Canada and Alaska. Also common in the Northeast and southward along the Appalachian mountain chain. Other populations occur in Florida, in the Ozarks, and in a number of western states.

Sound: Makes a variety of sounds, including snorts, cowlike moans, and growls.

On the CD
Moans and snorts of an adult

Range and Habitat: Widespread; found throughout most of North America. Frequents a variety of habitats, including dense forests prairies, and even city parks. Usually found near water. Very common in wooded swamps.

Sound: During squabbles or fights, makes whimpering or whining sounds, loud screeches or screams, and doglike barks. Distinctive throaty warbles are given when foraging at night.

On the CD
Barks, screeches, and whines given during a family squabble followed by the soft, throaty warbles of an individual

Range and Habitat: Found throughout the United States and southern Canada. Prefers the edges of fields and woods, but may be found in many different habitats. Finds shelter in natural cavities or undergound burrows.

Sound: Not very vocal, but makes high-pitched, whimpering squeals during courtship and other social encounters.

On the CD
Various high-pitched calls made by a pair (probably during courtship)

Range and Habitat: Found throughout most of Canada and much of the United States, with the exception of prairie areas and desert regions. Extremely aquatic, preferring rivers, lakes, and coastal wetlands.

Sound: Makes loud, airy snorts when moving about or feeding. Other common sounds include a grunting chuckle and birdlike chirps or peeps.

On the CD
Loud snorts and growls followed by throaty chuckles and peeps (from several individuals)

Range and Habitat: Found throughout most of the United States and the southern edge of Canada. Frequents a wide variety of habitats ranging from dense forest to desert and swampland. Solitary, elusive, and shy.

Sound: Usually quiet, but may produce snarling or gagging growls and snorts.

On the CD
Expressive growls made by
an individual

Range and Habitat: Our most familiar deer. Found throughout most of the United States and southern Canada. Especially abundant in farm country rich with woodland edges. A pest in many towns or suburban areas, where it eats shrubs and other ornamental vegetation.

Sound: Common alarm sound is a loud, airy snort or *whiew!*, sometimes accompanied by foot stomping. Fawns produce a distinctive mournful bleat, which alerts the doe to their whereabouts.

On the CD
Alarm snorts of an adult followed by nasal bleating calls of a fawn

Range and Habitat: A northern species frequenting forests, meadows, swamps, and tundra throughout most of Canada and the northern boreal forest regions of the United States. Often seen wading in water while feeding on marsh vegetation.

Sound: During rut, bull moose follow females and make low grunting sounds. Females often respond with drawn-out moans or moos similar to the sounds made by domestic cows.

On the CD
Grunts of male and moan of female given during courtship followed by typical mooing of two captive moose prior to being fed

Range and Habitat: Found throughout the eastern United States, across southern Canada, and into Washington and Oregon. Prefers forested regions and swamps, especially heavily wooded river bottomlands. Very common in the swampy woodlands of the Southeast.

Sound: Classic hoot pattern sounds like *who cooks for you . . . who cooks for you-all*. Other calls include a simple *whoo-ahhh* and a series of hoots that ascend in pitch and end with an accented hoot. Owls meeting in the dark often hoot excitedly, alternating and overlapping monkeylike calls in a distinctive manner. Fledglings beg for food with raspy screeches.

On the CD

Classic hooting followed by several other patterns (including two individuals hooting back and forth), ending with screeches of begging young

Note: *Whereas most of the species in this book are listed by family, the birds have been grouped more generally because of the large number of families to which they belong.*

Zenaida macroura

Range and Habitat: Common throughout the United States and along the southern edge of Canada. Frequents a wide variety of open habitats, including farmland, fields, suburban areas, and backyards.

Sound: The male's courtship call is a mournful coo sounding like *ooo-wah-hoo-oo-oo*. This call may be mistaken for the hooting of a distant owl. Another call is a short *ooo-waooh*. A distinctive whistling twitter can be made by the wings, most often as a dove takes flight or comes in for a landing.

On the CD
Typical cooing of one bird followed by coos and wing twitter of another

25. Great Horned Owl *Bubo virginianus*

Range and Habitat: Very widespread. Found throughout most of North America except fo northern arctic regions. Frequents a wide variety of habitats, including dense forest, dry desert, prairie, agricultural areas, and even suburban and city parks.

Sound: Typical adult hoot stays on the same pitch and sounds like *hoo, hoohoo, hoooo, hoooo*. Female's hoots are higher in pitch than the male's. Immatures make loud screeching sounds and hissing whistles. Like most other owls, snaps bill when alarmed.

On the CD
Hooting of adult pair at dawn followed by screeches, whistles, and bill-snapping of several different immature owls

Range and Habitat: Found throughout most of eastern and central United States. Common inhabitant of deciduous woodlands, farm groves, swamp forest, and suburban areas or city parks having lots of trees.

Sound: Has two common call types. One is an eerie, wavering whinny that rises and then falls in pitch. The other is a toadlike musical trill that usually stays on one pitch but may vary in tempo. Trills may be given alone or in alternation with whinny calls.

On the CD
Whinny calls and trills of an individual followed by trills of two additional birds

Range and Habitat: Common throughout most of the eastern United States and adjacent areas in Canada, but absent from much of the South. An isolated population occurs in the Southwest. Prefers rich, moist deciduous or mixed woodland habitats. (Note: In southern pinewoods, the Chuck-will's-widow, a close relative of the Whip-poor-will, is often heard. It sounds much like the Whip-poor-will, but its song has a noticeably different rhythm and accent.)

Sound: Familiar song is a wavering, whistled *whip-poor-will . . . whip-poor-will . . . whip-poor-will . . .* repeated for minutes on end at dusk or all through the night. A very soft *tuck* note precedes each song. A throaty *yaw-yaw-yaw-yaw* is given during social encounters.

On the CD
Typical songs of three different males, with throaty calls given at end

28. Red-tailed Hawk   *Buteo jamaicensis*

Range and Habitat: A widespread and well-known hawk. Breeds throughout most of North America except for northern arctic areas. Found in
open country, plains, prairies, woodland edges, mountains, and deserts.

Sound: The common call is a harsh, drawn-out scream with a distinctive
hissing quality likened to steam escaping: *pseeyerrrrr*. This call is the
familiar "eagle scream" heard in many movies. A whining, up-slurred
whistle is made by immatures and is also given by adults during
courtship: *kleee . . . kleee . . . klooeek . . . klooeek . . . klooeek . . .*

On the CD
Screeches of an individual followed
by various nasal whistles given by
several other birds

Range and Habitat: A common hawk of eastern deciduous and mixed woodlands, especially bottomland woods and swamps. Very vocal. More often heard than seen.

Sound: Primary call is a down-slurred scream, *kee-yer, kee-yer, kee-yer,* which is not nearly as hissy as the scream of the Red-tailed Hawk. Another call is a distinctive two-part *kick-uck, kick-uck, kick-uck* given during courtship flights.

On the CD
Typical *kee-yer* alarm calls (given near a nest) followed by *kick-uck* calls of individual (given in flight, probably during courtship)

Range and Habitat: A common woodland hawk found throughout most of eastern United States and adjacent Canada. Prefers deciduous or mixed forest. Often seen along forest edges or near clearings in the woods.

Sound: The call is a thin, hissing whistle or screech, *ptseeeeee*, quite unlike that of the Red-tailed Hawk.

On the CD
Hissing alarm whistles given
near nest

31. Northern Flicker

Colaptes auratus

Range and Habitat: Common and widespread. Found throughout most of North America except for northern arctic regions. Prefers open woodlands but may be found in any habitat with trees. Frequents surburban areas where it may be seen looking for insects on lawns.

Sound: Most obvious call is rapid sequence of notes sounding like *ki-ki-ki-ki-ki-ki-ki*, often lasting for eight seconds or longer. Another call is a nasal, downslurred *peeough* or *peeyerr*. Flickers also drum on wood, producing an even-tempo drumbeat that lasts about two seconds.

On the CD
Ki-ki-ki-ki calls, *peeough* calls, and drumming

Range and Habitat: Found throughout most of the eastern United States and adjacent areas in Canada, and also ranges westward across Canada and down the Pacific coast states to California. Absent from northern Canada and Alaska. Prefers dense, mature forest, but is becoming common in surburbs and second-growth woodlands.

Sound: Has a distinctive whinnylike outburst of notes that usually drops in volume and pitch at the end. Another common call is a long series of clucking notes delivered at a variable rate: *cuk, cuk . . . cuk . . . cuck . . . cuk, cuk . . .* This call is similar to the Northern Flicker's call, but is lower in pitch and more musical. Drumming is loud and resonant and trails off in volume at the end.

On the CD

Two whinnylike outbursts, two series of *cuk* calls, and two examples of drumming

Range and Habitat: Found throughout most of the eastern United States but is absent from northern areas (although in recent years this species has been expanding its range northward). Very common in southeastern swamp forests and pinewoods. Also frequents suburbs and city parks.

Sound: Primary call is a vibrant rolling *querrrr . . . querrrr*, often given in twos or threes. Other calls include a slowly repeated *chi* or *chit*, which is sometimes delivered as a rapid outburst of calls. The drumming has an even tempo and lasts about a second.

On the CD
Typical *querrr* calls, *chit* calls and outbursts, and drumming

Range and Habitat: Found throughout the eastern and central United States, but uncommon and local in many areas. Prefers open woods, forest edges, orchards, and other habitats with large, scattered trees. Avoids unbroken forest.

Sound: Primary call is a tremulous *qweer*, more nasal and higher in pitch than the similar call of the Red-bellied Woodpecker. Other calls include a series of harsh *churr*s often given in flight, and a dry rattle. The drumming has an even tempo and lasts about a second.

On the CD
Qweer calls, drumming, and harsh flight *churr* of one bird followed by typical calls and drumming of another, ending with rattle calls given by a bird near its nest at dusk

Range and Habitat: One of our most well-known woodpeckers. Ranges across most of North America but is absent from northern Canada. Favors open as well as dense woodlands, farmland, and suburbs. A common visitor to bird feeders.

Sound: Primary call is a sharp *peek!* that is usually repeated a number of times. Another call is a sudden outburst of notes that drop in pitch at the end, sounding like the whinny of a miniature horse. The drumming has an even tempo and lasts a second or less.

On the CD
Peek! calls followed by typical whinnylike outburst and drumming

36. American Robin *Turdus migratorius*

Range and Habitat: A well-known and much-loved songbird that is found in many environments throughout North America, from dense forest to open farmland. Frequents residential areas and city parks, where it may be seen on lawns, searching for earthworms.

Sound: The male's melodic, caroling song is a variable series of wavering, whistled phrases sounding like *cheerily, cheeriup, cheerio, cheerily*. Short pauses occur between songs. The most common call is a high-pitched, whinnylike outburst of notes. Alarm calls given near the nest sound like *peek! . . . peek! . . . tut, tut, tut . . . peek! . . . tut, tut . . .*

On the CD

Typical song sequence followed by whinny calls, then *peek!* and *tut* calls given near a nest

Range and Habitat: A well-known songbird with striking color and beautiful song. Common throughout most of the eastern and central United States. Also found in the Southwest. Frequents a variety of habitats, including woodland edges, overgrown fields, brushy borders, suburban areas, and city parks.

Sound: Bright and melodic song is a series of slurred, whistled phrases that are repeated several times and then varied. Each individual has a vocabulary of several phrase types that it combines into different songs: *purdy, purdy, purdy, whoit-whoit-whoit-whoit* or *purdy, purdy, teer-doe, teer-doe, teer-doe* (or any of a wide variety of similar themes). The common call is a metallic *chip*.

On the CD
Two songs of one male, one song each from two different males, and typical alarm *chip*s.

Range and Habitat: A colorful and vocal songbird. Ranges throughout most of the eastern United States and into adjacent areas in Canada. May be found in open woodlands, riverine forests, orchards, city parks, and gardens.

Sound: Song is a sequence of bright, slurred whistles, sometimes including harsh or raspy notes. Each male has only one song type that he repeats over and over, but song is highly variable from male to male. Simple whistles are often given between songs. Calls include a nasal *jeet-jeet* and a rattling chatter.

On the CD
Songs and whistles of three different males followed by nasal calls and rattling chatter

Range and Habitat: Found throughout much of the United States and southern Canada, but is generally absent from the Southwest and Pacific States. Prefers shrubby or brushy areas such as woodland edges, hedgerows, overgrown fields, shrub swamps, and suburban backyards. More often heard than seen.

Sound: Song is a long series of variable squeaky whistled phrases; the male sings unique phrase after unique phrase without ever seeming to repeat himself (unlike the Brown Thrasher and Northern Mockingbird). Common call is a catlike mewing note, which is how the catbird got its name. Alarm call given near the nest is a throaty *kwut, kwut, kwut, kwut . . .*

On the CD
Typical song sequence followed by loud *mew* calls and throaty *kwut* notes (given near nest)

Range and Habitat: Found throughout most of eastern and central United States and adjacent areas in Canada. Frequents thickets and other brushy or shrubby areas. Often remains hidden, but may suddenly appear at the top of a tree singing with tail tucked in a downward position.

Sound: Song is a long series of melodious whistled phrases, each repeated two times (or sometimes three or four times) before switching to the next phrase. Lower in pitch and more melodic than the Gray Catbird's song. Calls include a sharp *smack!* and a harsh *chjjjjj*.

On the CD
Typical song sequence followed by *smack!* calls and harsh *chjjjjj* call

41. Northern Mockingbird *Mimus polyglottos*

Range and Habitat: Found throughout most of the United States, though rare in the northern central and northwestern states. Favors open shrubby areas, woodland edges, rural and suburban thickets, and farmland.

Sound: Melodic song is an extended series of robust whistled phrases, each repeated three to ten times or more. Songs often include striking imitations of the sounds made by other birds. Calls include a raspy *chjjjjj* and a sharp *chewk*.

On the CD
Typical song sequence followed by raspy *chjjjjj* and sharp *chewk* calls.

Range and Habitat: A well-known feeder bird. Ranges across northern United States and throughout much of Canada, but does not occur in the northern tundra regions. Found in a variety of habitats, including mixed and deciduous forest, farmland, suburban woodlots, city parks, and backyards.

Sound: Song is a clear two-note whistle that drops in pitch: *fee-beee* or *fee-bee-eee* (the last note is usually double-pulsed). The familiar *chicka-dee-dee-dee-dee* call gives this bird its name. Other calls include a simple *tsit* and high-pitched gargles.

On the CD

Whistled *fee-bee-ee* song followed by *chick-a-dee-dee-dee* calls and various high-pitched notes.

Range and Habitat: A southerly chickadee, found throughout the Southeast and west to Texas and Oklahoma. Overlaps with Black-capped Chickadee along the northern edge of its range, from New Jersey west to Illinois and Missouri. Found in mixed and deciduous woods as well as in pine-oak habitats.

Sound: Classic song is a series of about four high-pitched whistles sounding like *fee-bee-fee-bay*. Other song types may include five or more whistles. Primary call sounds like *chicka-dee-dee-dee-dee*, with the *dee* notes being repeated more times and more rapidly than those of the Black-capped Chickadee.

On the CD
Whistled *fee-bee-fee-bay* song followed by variant song type and some typical calls

Range and Habitat: Abundant throughout most of the eastern United States and as far west as Texas. Absent from northern areas. A woodland species favoring deciduous forest. Often seen and heard in trees around houses in suburban areas. A common feeder bird.

Sound: Song is a short series of down-slurred whistles sounding like *peter-peter-peter* or *peerda-peerda-peerda*. Neighboring males often match song types as they sing back and forth. Another special song sounds like *keep-her . . . keep-her . . .* Calls include a high, metallic *tseet* and a chickadeelike *tseet-jway-jway-jway*.

On the CD

Songs of several different males followed by *tseet* notes, *keep-her* song, and *tseet-jway* and similar calls

Range and Habitat: A well-known feeder bird. Found throughout much of the United States and the southern edge of Canada. Prefers deciduous and mixed woodlands. Commonly seen in suburban areas and city parks.

Sound: The male's song is a vibrant series of nasal notes sounding like *hey-hey-hey-hey-hey-hey* and heard from midwinter through spring. Common call is a nasal *ank* or *ank-ank*. Soft *ik* notes are given while bird is moving about and foraging.

On the CD
Nasal songs of two different males followed by typical *yank-yank* calls and soft *ik* notes

Range and Habitat: Found throughout most of the United States and southern Canada, but does not breed in the southern states. Common and
abundant in rural and suburban areas. Frequents woodland edges,
brushy habitats, orchards, farmyards, and city parks.

Sound: Song is a rich, bubbling chatter that starts with soft notes, rises in
volume and pitch, then cascades down in pitch at the end. Common
calls, usually given in alarm, include simple *chit* notes, a rattling series of
*chit*s, and a harsh rattling *churrrrrr*.

On the CD
Typical songs followed by two
examples of rattling calls

47. Carolina Wren
Thryothorus ludovicianus

Range and Habitat: Ranges throughout much of the eastern United States but is absent or rare in most of the northern states. Common in the brushy undergrowth of deciduous or mixed woods, and along forest edges. Frequents suburban areas.

Sound: Song is a loud repeated series of ringing notes that sound like *tea-kettle, tea-kettle, tea-kettle, tea-kettle*. Males have a number of different song types in their repertoire. They usually repeat one song for a minute or longer before switching to another type. Common call in northern part of range is a down-slurred *cheeeer*. Gives a ringing *pdink!* in the South.

On the CD
Songs of two males (both switch song types) followed by *cheeeer* and *pdink!* calls

Range and Habitat: A well-known eastern and central songbird ranging into adjacent areas of Canada. Frequents a variety of woodland habitats, preferring oak, beech, or pine woods over much of its range. Common around towns and in suburban areas. Aggressive and dominant around bird feeders.

Sound: Blue Jays make an incredible variety of sounds, many piping and musical in quality. Common call is a harsh and vibrant *jaay* or *jaay-jaay*. Also produces a melodic *tool-ool*, a squeaky *wheedlee*, and various odd clicking sounds. Whining, nasal notes are given as family members forage together in trees.

On the CD
Eight examples of various call types

Range and Habitat: Found throughout eastern and central United States and in Canada, where it ranges as far north as the Northwest Territories. Common along streams, around farmhouses and barns, along woodland edges, and wherever else it can find ledges and other protected surfaces on which to build its mud nest.

Sound: Species is named after song, a rough alternation of two similar song types having slightly different endings: *fee-beee* (buzzy ending) and *fee-britit* (liquid ending). Common call is a high-pitched *chip*.

On the CD
Typical song sequence followed by *chip* notes

Range and Habitat: Found in moist, deciduous woodlands and swamps throughout the eastern United States and adjacent areas in Canada. Often heard singing in suburban woodlots.

Sound: Beautiful flutelike song sounds like *ee-oh-lay-oh-weee* or *ee-oh-leee*. Several low-pitched introductory notes are followed by a musical phrase that terminates with a high trill. Males have a number of different songs in their repertoire and they almost never repeat the same song twice in a row. Calls include short volleys of throaty *tut* notes or liquid *wit* notes.

On the CD

Song sequence followed by two examples of calls

Range and Habitat: Familiar and widespread. Ranges across most of North America except in far northern areas. Breeds in freshwater marshes, shrub swamps, and upland hayfields. Flies to fields and other open areas to feed.

Sound: Male's song is a loud, gurgling *conk-la-reee* or *o-ka-leee*. Common call is a sharp *tchack*. Alarm call given around nest is a piercing, down-slurred whistle: *see-yeee*.

On the CD
Typical *conk-la-reee* songs followed by *tchack* notes and alarm whistles

Range and Habitat: A common and widespread member of the warbler family. Found throughout most of the United States and southern Canada. Frequents a variety of open or brushy habitats, ranging from overgrown fields and hedgerows to the shrubby edges of marshes and swamps.

Sound: Lively song is a high-pitched series of repeated phrases sounding like *witchety-witchety-witchey-witch*. Common calls include a rattling *tschat* and, more rarely, a sharp *steek*.

On the CD

Two songs each of two males, one song of another male, and rattling *tschat*s and *steek* calls

Range and Habitat: Common throughout most of eastern United States. A resident of overgrown fields, open woodlands with dense undergrowth, brushy forest edges, and streamside thickets.

Sound: Song is variable, but most typical pattern is comprised of two short, whistled notes followed by a high-pitched trill: *drink-your-teeeeee*. Most common call is a distinctive up-slurred nasal *che-weee*.

On the CD

Two songs each of three different males followed by nasal *che-weee* calls

54. American Goldfinch *Carduelis tristis*

Range and Habitat: A well-known songbird of open country. Ranges across most of the United States and southern Canada. Frequents croplands, weedy fields, second-growth woodlands, and roadsides. A common feeder bird.

Sound: Gives volleys of sweet notes sounding like *per-tee-tee-tee* or *perchickory* as it swoops down and then up in flight. In spring, males sing excited warbling songs that are rambling and continuous. During nesting in midsummer, songs become more precise with clear pauses in between. Common call is a nasal, ascending *su-weet*.

On the CD
Perchickory flight calls, extended song, several short songs, and *su-weet* calls

Range and Habitat: A common and widespread sparrow, ranging through-out most of North America but absent from the far north (it winters in the southern states but does not breed there). Prefers semi-open areas, including dense shrubbery at the edges of fields, hedgerows, yard and garden habitats, streamside thickets, and marsh edges.

Sound: Lively song begins with several bright notes followed by a sequence of warbles and trills that varies considerably among males (in spite of this variation, it is easy to learn the overall pattern or "gestalt" of the species song). Common call is a nasal *chimp*.

On the CD
Four song types from one male's repertoire followed by nasal *chimp* calls

Range and Habitat: Common and widespread, ranging throughout most of North America but absent from the far north. Found in grassy areas, open woodlands, parks, suburbs, and backyards.

Sound: Typical song is a rapid trill lasting several seconds and often having a dry, buzzy quality (the songs of some males are more tinkling and melodic). At dawn, sings a special song composed of short trills of variable length given at a lively pace.

On the CD

Two songs of one male followed by one song of another, then dawn song

Range and Habitat: Breeds in swamps, lakes, rivers, bayous, and marshes of the southern states, from Virginia south to Florida and west to Arkansas, Louisiana, and Texas. Grows up to sixteen feet long.

Sound: Males make low-pitched, bellowing growls or roars during breeding season. When annoyed, alligators respond with drawn-out hisses or snorts. Young alligators make distinctive squeaking nasal grunts.

On the CD
Loud roars of a male, hiss and snort of an alarmed individual, and nasal calls of young

58. Timber Rattlesnake

Crotalus horridus

Range and Habitat: A widespread eastern rattlesnake, ranging from Texas to the Carolinas in the South and northward to Wisconsin and the Northeastern states. Timber Rattlesnakes often den in great numbers during the winter among rocky ledges near woods. Favors heavily forested areas. Though poisonous, this species is reasonably docile and does not usually pose a threat to humans.

Sound: When alarmed, all rattlesnakes produce a distinctive high-pitched buzzing or rattling sound made by vibrating the horny "rattles" on their tails. Take notice if you hear this sound—you don't want to inadvertently step on a rattlesnake!

On the CD
Typical rattling

59. Spring Peeper   *Pseudacris crucifer*

Range and Habitat: Widespread and abundant throughout the eastern half of the United States and southern Canada. Breeds all spring in a variety of wetlands, including pools, ponds, lakes, and ditches.

Sound: Males make loud, piercing, birdlike *peeps* that may sound like sleigh bells when heard at a distance. Neighboring males often alternate calls in a regular fashion. Groups form deafening choruses that make one's ears flutter uncontrollably at close range. If a male is approached by a rival, he responds with a short stuttering trill that rises in pitch and sounds similar to the call of the Western Chorus Frog.

On the CD
Two males alternating calls, a huge chorus, and stuttering trills given during interaction

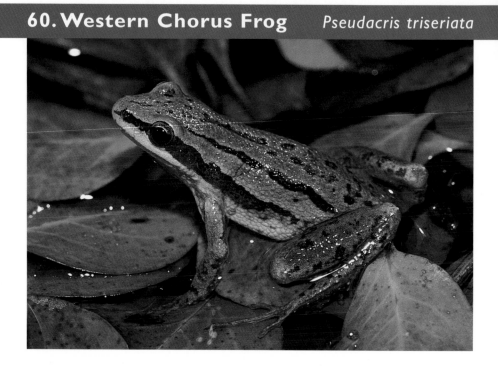

Range and Habitat: The Western Chorus Frog and related species such as the Southeastern Chorus Frog (*P. feriarum*) and Boreal Chorus Frog (*P. maculata*), are found throughout much of the eastern and central United States and central Canada. All are early spring breeders, preferring shallow temporary wetlands such as roadside ditches, the flooded margins of fields, and the like, but they may sometimes be found in deeper woodland pools.

Sound: Primary call of male is a rapid series of metallic, creaking clicks that rise in pitch, much like the sound made by rubbing a finger across the stiff teeth of a comb: *crrreeeek . . . crrreeeek . . . crrreeeek . . .* Neighboring males often alternate calls.

On the CD
Typical creaking calls in a small chorus

Range and Habitat: Widespread and abundant throughout most of eastern United States, but notably absent from the Northeast, the Appalachian mountains, and the extreme Southeast. Breeds from late winter into summer. Calls from open grassy edges of ponds, lakes, creeks, and swampy areas.

Sound: A series of metallic notes that sound like two small glass marbles being tapped together: _giiick-giiick-giiick-giiick_ . . . Notes are usually given in a long series that starts out slow, speeds up in tempo, and then slows down at the end. Large choruses can be deafening at close range.

On the CD
Calls of several individuals followed by a larger chorus

Range and Habitat: Common in the northeastern and northern central states, and also ranges southward from Missouri to Louisiana and Texas. Absent from the Southeast. Generally non-overlapping with look-alike species Cope's Gray Treefrog. (The two species were long considered one and are best distinguished by their calls.) Breeds from late spring into summer in ponds and pools surrounded by shrubs or trees.

Sound: Call is a short, melodic trill lasting about one-half second and repeated every few seconds. When approached by a rival, a male may respond with squeaky chirps or yelps that signify aggression.

On the CD

Several males calling (with Green Frogs), an individual calling (with Spring Peepers), and a chorus with prominent aggressive chirps

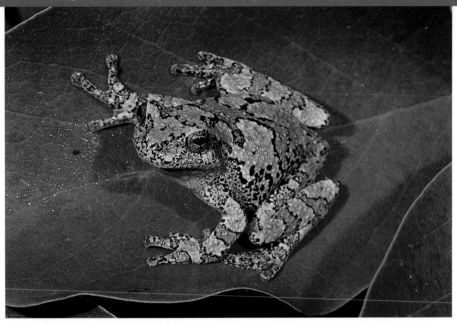

Range and Habitat: Found throughout much of eastern United States, but absent from the Northeast. Generally non-overlapping with look-alike species Gray Treefrog. Breeds from late spring into summer in shallow ponds, pools, and ditches surrounded by shrubs or trees.

Sound: Call of male is a short rattling trill, like that of the Gray Treefrog but not nearly as melodic.

On the CD
One small chorus followed by another

Range and Habitat: An abundant southern treefrog that frequents a variety of wetland habitats. Found throughout the South, from Florida to Texas, north to Missouri in the central region, and north to Delaware along the Atlantic coast. Breeds in stillwater swamps, marshes, and ponds.

Sound: Breeding call is a harsh, nasal *quank* repeated about once per second. From a distance, calls may sound bell-like, which accounts for the nickname of "cowbell frog." Aggressive call given during encounters is a hoarse, garbled *quarrr-quarrr-quarrr* repeated quickly.

On the CD
Closeup of individual (with Pig Frogs and Bullfrog), two individuals interacting with one giving aggression calls, and another small chorus (with Pig Frogs)

65. Green Frog *Rana clamitans*

Range and Habitat: Abundant throughout most of eastern United States and southeastern Canada. Found along the edges of ponds, lakes, streams, and other permanent bodies of water. Breeds from spring to late summer and calls from shoreline or from floating vegetation.

Sound: Breeding call of the male is an explosive, throaty *gunk!* or *gung!* that resembles the sound made by plucking a loose banjo string. Calls often delivered in a series that drops slightly in pitch and volume: *Goonk!-gunk!-gunk!* During encounters, may give several stuttering guttural calls followed by a single staccato *gunk!*

On the CD
Typical *gunk!* calls of a small chorus with stuttering calls at end (and barely audible Spring Peeper)

Range and Habitat: Our largest native frog, ranging throughout eastern and central North America, with patchy distribution in the West. Found in permanent lakes, ponds, and streams. Calls from shallow water along shorelines or from offshore patches of floating or emergent vegetation. May be heard from May to August in the North and late winter to autumn in the South.

Sound: Breeding call of male is a series of loud, resonant bass notes sounding like *rumm . . . rumm . . . rumm . . .* or else a stuttering *ru-u-u-umm . . . ru-u-u-umm . . .* Often verbalized as "jug-o-rum," it resembles the bellowing of a bull. An abrupt, spitlike *phphoot!* is given during aggressive encounters.

On the CD
Calling of a dense group followed by a closeup of one individual and several aggressive *phphoot!* calls (with Southern Cricket Frog)

Range and Habitat: A northern species, found in the northeastern and northern central United States, and throughout most of Canada and Alaska. Prefers moist wooded areas. Breeds after the first spring rains, sometimes with snow still on the ground. Males gather in woodland pools and roadside ditches and call excitedly while floating on the water. Breeding only lasts a week or two if suitable weather persists.

Sound: Breeding call is a ducklike quacking or cackling, usually consisting of several harsh notes given in rapid succession: *cack-a-hack* or *cack-a-hack-a-hack*.

On the CD
Cackling calls given in a small, cool chorus followed by a larger, warmer chorus (with Spring Peeper)

Range and Habitat: Found throughout much of eastern United States, but absent from the extreme Southeast. Breeds in lakes, ponds, streams, bogs, swamps, springs, and in the twilight pools at cave entrances. Heard primarily in the spring, but may sound off in early summer in northern areas.

Sound: Call is a harsh nasal snore of about two seconds' duration. Males sometimes call while submerged. Garbled, throaty notes are occasionally given singly, perhaps during aggressive encounters.

On the CD
Typical snores

Range and Habitat: Ranges across northern United States and southern Canada and southward to Arizona and New Mexico in the West. Breeds along vegetated margins of ponds, lakes, and streams. May be heard calling both day and night during the first warm spells of spring.

Sound: Breeding call is a rattling snore lasting about two and a half seconds and followed by a series of grunting chuckles. It is distinct from the Pickerel Frog's, which has a more nasal snore and does not include the chuckling sounds.

On the CD

Typical snores and grunting chuckles of an individual (with barely audible Spring Peeper)

Range and Habitat: Found throughout the southern states from Florida to Texas. Ranges north to Missouri, Illinois, and Indiana and along the Atlantic coast to Long Island. Breeds in spring in the northern part of its range but may be heard throughout the year in southern areas.

Sound: Primary call, which is repeated several times in rapid succession, consists of a series of five or more guttural notes delivered as a stutter that is usually too fast to count: *chu-hu-hu-hu-huck, chu-hu-hu-hu-huck, chu-hu-hu-hu-huck . . .* At high temperatures, this call is delivered at a more rapid rate. A series of squeaky grunts usually follow each outburst of chuckling calls.

On the CD
Guttural chuckles of a cool frog (with Spring Peeper) followed by faster chuckles of a warmer frog (with Green Treefrog and Southern Cricket Frog)

Range and Habitat: The common "warty toad" of the East. Found through-out most of eastern United States and Canada, but absent from the extreme South and Southeast. Frequents a variety of habitats, from urban and suburban areas to farm country and deep forest. Breeds from April to June in the North and as early as January in the South.

Sound: Breeding call is a long, dreamlike, musical trill lasting from up to thirty seconds or more. Each male in a chorus sings on a slightly differ-ence pitch, with males alternating and overlapping their calls in a pleas-ing manner. When mounted by another male, responds with distinctive squeaks or chirps that stimulate the offender to let go. Hybridizes with Fowler's Toad; hybrid individuals have intermediate calls that are some-where between the American's long, musical trill and the short, abrasive call of the Fowler's.

On the CD
Typical melodic trills heard in small chorus followed by loud release calls (with Spring Peeper)

Range and Habitat: Easily confused with the American Toad. Found through most of eastern United States, but absent from parts of the Northeast, the Southeast, and the upper Midwest. Prefers sandy habitats around the shores of lakes, ponds, and rivers. Breeds mostly from February through May.

Sound: Primary call is a buzzy, nasal trill lasting from one to five seconds: *waaaaaaaa!* Sounds somewhat like a baby crying. Hybridizes with the American Toad; hybrid individuals have calls intermediate between the two species.

On the CD
Nasal calls of several individuals (with Gray Treefrog), followed by deafening chorus

Range and Habitat: The common toad of the southern coastal plain region. Found from southeastern Virginia all the way to eastern Louisiana. Heard from March to June, especially after rains. Breeds in ponds, pools, and ditches, usually near forest.

Sound: A high-pitched trill lasting about five to ten seconds. Sounds similar to the trill of the American Toad, but not as melodic and higher in pitch. Considerable dissonance occurs in choruses when the loud calls of individuals overlap.

On the CD

Typical trills of two individuals
(with Green Treefrog)

Range and Habitat: A southern species, ranging from Maryland and Virginia west to Missouri and southward to the Gulf states. Found in a variety of habitats but prefers sandy soils. May be heard from spring to autumn, after heavy rains, in ponds, lakes, pools, and ditches.

Sound: Breeding call is a buzzy, nasal *waaaaaaa!* lasting from one to several seconds. Sounds like the call of the Fowler's Toad, but is shorter in duration, more buzzy, and sometimes preceded by a soft squeak or peep. Another call is a harsh, throaty *brrrrrrr*, apparently given when males have aggressive interactions.

On the CD
Nasal *waaaaa!* calls of several individuals with throaty *burrrr* calls evident near end

75. Eastern Spadefoot
Scaphiopus holbrookii

Range and Habitat: Primarily southeastern in distribution, but ranges northward into southern Illinois, Indiana, and Ohio, and along the Atlantic coast to Massachusetts. Prefers habitats with dry, loose soils where it can burrow underground. An explosive breeder, it can be heard calling from temporary pools for two or three days after heavy rains. Breeds during the summer in the North and anytime during the year in the South.

Sound: Breeding call is an explosive, nasal utterance, usually down-slurred and sounding like a person vomiting: *errrrrah!*

On the CD
Typical nasal calls given in a small chorus

Range and Habitat: An odd-looking cricket adapted for digging burrows. Found throughout the eastern and central United States. Lives along the margins of lakes, streams, and ponds, and also in low mucky habitats. Sings in the spring in the South and later in the summer in the northern part of its range. Most often heard in late afternoon and early evening.

Sound: The song of the mole cricket is a low-pitched series of brief trills or chirps given at a rate of two to three per second. Males chirp from within burrows, often with closed entrances, making the source of the sound difficult to locate.

On the CD
Chirping of warm cricket followed by chirping of a cooler one with call variation near end

Range and Habitat: A large black cricket that often makes its way into houses in the autumn. Ranges throughout much of the United States and southernmost Canada but is absent from the Southeast. Prefers open, grassy areas. The Fall Field Cricket begins singing in late summer and may be heard until early winter, especially on warm sunny days. The related Spring Field Cricket (*Gryllus veletis*) looks and sounds the same as the Fall Field Cricket, but is heard from spring into midsummer.

Sound: A quintessential chirping cricket, giving a regular series of high-pitched chirps (in actuality, brief trills) at a rate of about two per second.

On the CD
Typical chirping

Range and Habitat: A common ground cricket found throughout most of eastern and central United States. Absent from the southernmost states. Often heard calling in grassy areas such as lawns and meadows. Often mistaken for "baby crickets" because of their small size—less than $^1\!/_2$ inch long.

Sound: A high-pitched melodic trill given at a rate that is a little too fast to count (about fifteen pulses per second). The sweet quality and rapid rate of the trill allow this species to be distinguished from other look-alike ground crickets.

On the CD
Trilling of cool cricket followed by trilling of a warmer one (with calls of Gray Catbird)

Range and Habitat: Found throughout most of eastern United States but is absent from the extreme Southeast and from northern areas. A forest dweller inhabiting the leaf litter, it is common in oak woods.

Sound: A sweet, high-pitched trill given almost slow enough to count (about eight pulses per second). Easily confused with the trill of the Allard's Ground Cricket, but noticeably slower at any given temperature (nearly all insect songs speed up as the temperature rises).

On the CD
Tinkling trill of an individual

Range and Habitat: Widespread, ranging over most of the United States and extreme southeastern Canada. Found in grass or among leaves, often in ditches along roads, but also in lawns or around houses.

Sound: A very rapid buzzing trill (seventy to eighty pulses per second) that is not nearly as melodic as the songs of the Allard's and Tinkling ground crickets. The song tends to speed up and slow down, giving it a stumbling quality.

On the CD
Buzzy trill with stops and starts

Range and Habitat: Common in the Northeast, upper Midwest, southern Canada, and over much of the West. Often heard singing in wet, grassy areas near water.

Sound: A chirping ground cricket, giving a long-continued series of high-pitched chirps (brief trills, actually) at a rate of about two chirps per second. Sounds similar to the Fall Field Cricket, but is more rhythmic and not as strong.

On the CD
Typical chirping of individual

Range and Habitat: A common, widespread, and familiar tree cricket found throughout much of North America but absent from most of the southeastern states. Sings from shrubby or viney patches, often at the edges of fields and along roadsides.

Sound: Gives melodic and fairly low-pitched chirps at a rate of around two to three per second. Sounds similar to the Northern Mole Cricket, but higher in pitch. Neighboring males often sing in unison. Referred to as the "temperature cricket" because a close approximation of the temperature in Fahrenheit can be determined by counting the number of chirps that occur in fifteen seconds and then adding forty.

On the CD
Chirping of a cool cricket followed by chirping of a warmer one

Range and Habitat: Common throughout much of eastern and central United States, but absent from northern areas. Frequents brushy or shrubby areas along roadsides or in overgrown fields and woodland understory, where it calls from fairly low perches.

Sound: Male's song is a loud, rapid, melodic trill that is much too fast to count (about fifty pulses per second).

On the CD

Loud trill of individual
(with Northern True Katydid)

Range and Habitat: A northern species, ranging from the Northeast and southeastern Canada through the upper Midwest. Commonly found in overgrown meadows and prairie grasslands. Often associated with goldenrods and blackberry vines.

Sound: A rapid melodic trill (about fifty pulses per second), somewhat thinner and higher in pitch than the similarly paced trill of the Broad-winged Tree Cricket.

On the CD

Continuous trill of individual

85. Common Meadow Katydid *Orchelimum vulgare*

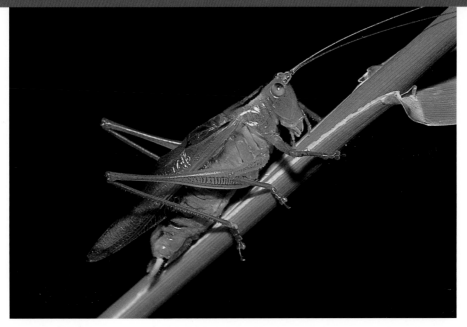

Range and Habitat: A very widespread species found over much of eastern and central United States, extending just barely into Canada at the northern end of its range. Found mostly in grassy meadows or the grassy margins of roads and fields.

Sound: A series of high-pitched, sibilant clicks or zips followed by a grating buzz that starts soft and quickly grows louder: *zt . . . zt . . . zt . . . zeeeeeeeeee*. Heard both day and night.

On the CD
Typical calling

86. Handsome Meadow Katydid *Orchelimum pulchellum*

Range and Habitat: One of our most beautiful meadow katydids. Found along the coastal plain from Delaware south to Florida and west to Louisiana. Often found on emergent vegetation in wet areas such as the edges of lakes and streams, wet meadows, and other open, swampy areas.

Sound: Song is a rapid series of high zips followed by a grating buzz, like a speeded-up version of the Common Meadow Katydid's song. Heard both day and night.

On the CD
Typical *zt-zt-zt-zeeeee* calls (with Northern True Katydid, various other insects, and Green Frog)

Range and Habitat: An abundant conehead of northern areas, ranging from the northeastern United States and southeastern Canada westward to the prairie states. Commonly heard in meadows with tall grass and along roadsides.

Sound: A long-continued series of high-pitched, lispy notes given at a rate of about eight to eleven pulses per second: *tsee-tsee-tsee-tsee-tsee* . . . Males usually call from about midway up the grass blades, but sometimes may call from the ground. Heard from late afternoon into the night.

On the CD
Typical calling of a cool conehead followed by more rapid calling of a warm one

Range and Habitat: A common conehead of the central United States, ranging from Nebraska to Pennsylvania along the northern edge of its range and southward to Louisiana and Texas. Absent from the Southeast. Found in shrubby thickets and overgrown fields.

Sound: A series of loud, high-pitched, raspy buzzes, each lasting about two seconds and separated by one or two seconds of silence: *zeeeee . . . zeeeee . . . zeeeee . . . zeeeee . . .*

On the CD
Typical loud buzzes of an individual (various insects in background)

Range and Habitat: Ranges from Connecticut to Kansas along the northern edge of its range, and southward to the Gulf States. Absent from the extreme Southeast. Calls from moist thickets, cattail marshes, and other shrubby habitats.

Sound: A series of loud, high-pitched, metallic buzzes given at a rate of around three buzzes per second. Slightly more musical in quality than the sounds made by other coneheads: *zeet, zeet, zeet, zeet, zeet, zeet . . .*

On the CD
Typical repeated metallic buzzes
(various insects in background)

Range and Habitat: Found from Connecticut to Nebraska along the northern edge of its range and southward to the Gulf states. Heard calling in grassy or weedy areas, old fields, roadsides, and the edges of marshes.

Sound: A continuous high-pitched metallic, crackling or sputtering buzz that is similar to the sound made by a shorting electric line. Quite unlike the calls of the other coneheads.

On the CD
Typical sputtering buzz
(with Northern True Katydid)

Range and Habitat: Our most familiar and vocal katydid. Found over most of the eastern United States, though it is absent from the north woods. Found primarily in deciduous forest habitats, especially oak woods, where large numbers may call from high in the trees.

Sound: Call is a loud vibrant buzz. Northern populations typically deliver calls in two-note or three-note groupings: *chee-chee* or *chee-chee-chee* (which some listeners think sounds like *ka-ty-did . . . ka-ty-did*). In contrast, southeastern populations deliver calls in more rapid groups of four notes sounding like a short rattle: *ch-ch-ch-ch . . . ch-ch-ch-ch . . .*

On the CD
Two-part and three-part calls of an individual from the northern population followed by four-part calls of an individual from the southeastern population

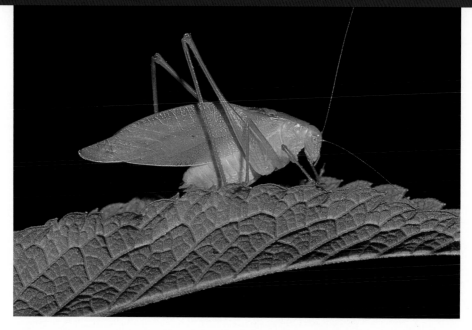

Range and Habitat: A northern species, ranging from southern Maine to southern Wisconsin and southward to Tennessee. Sings from tall weeds, shrubs, and small trees in overgrown fields and along roadsides.

Sound: Call is a series of high-pitched rattles. Usually begins with a number of short rattles lasting about one second each and then finally terminating with an extended rattle of five to ten seconds' duration.

On the CD
Typical calling with brief and extended rattles

Range and Habitat: Found throughout most of eastern and central United States, as well as extreme southeastern Canada. Absent from most of Florida. Calls from tall vegetation, shrubs, and small trees in overgrown fields and along woodland edges.

Sound: Distinctive call is a buzzy *zit-zitick* given once every five seconds or so.

On the CD
Repeated *zit-zituck* calls
(with various insects)

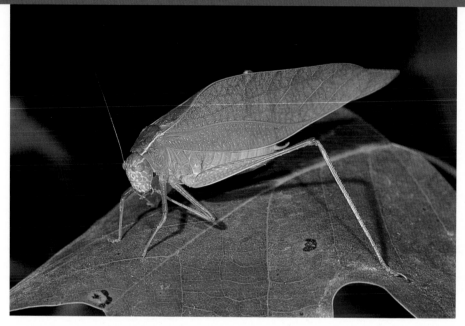

Range and Habitat: Found throughout most of eastern United States, but absent from northernmost regions. Also ranges from Texas into the Southwest. Primarily a deciduous forest species, it is often heard singing from high in the trees.

Sound: Has two call types. One is a rapid series of high-pitched clicks or *tip*s: *tip-tip-tip-tip-tip* . . . The other is a lisping *zeet* given once every two or three seconds.

On the CD

Three different click-series followed by lisping *zeet* calls

Range and Habitat: Ranges from New Jersey to Missouri along the northern part of its range, and southward to the Gulf states. Prefers forest habitats. Usually calls from high in the treetops.

Sound: Rattling call is a rapid volley of four or five high-pitched lispy notes: *zt-zt-zt-zt-zt*. Similar to the song of southeastern Northern True Katydids, but higher in pitch.

On the CD
Typical call volleys (with Northern True Katydid and other insects)

Range and Habitat: A northern species ranging from the northeastern United States and southeastern Canada westward to Alberta and Wyoming. Found in overgrown fields, especially where there are lots of shrubs and goldenrod.

Sound: Call is a buzzing *zick* given in a measured series that increases in loudness from beginning to end. This katydid actually seems to count. A call sequence often begins with a group of two rather soft *zick* notes. About five seconds later a longer series of three calls are given. This is followed by yet a longer series of four calls, then yet another series or two, until a final group of seven or eight calls marks the end of the sequence. Several minutes later the insect may initiate a new call sequence.

On the CD
Typical call series progressing from two soft buzzes to seven loud ones

Range and Habitat: One of the most commonly heard cicadas in the eastern and central United States. Uncommon in northern areas. Prefers deciduous forest where it calls from high in the trees.

Sound: A single call lasts about ten seconds. It begins as a soft, pulsating buzz that gradually increases in loudness with intensified pulsation, and then finally trails off at the end: *ZEE-uhhh-ZEE-uhhh-ZEE-uhhh-ZEE-uhhh . . .*

On the CD
Two typical undulating calls

Range and Habitat: Found throughout much of eastern United States but is absent from northern areas. Commonly heard in shrub swamps and also in overgrown fields and meadows, where they may be seen flying from perch to perch and calling.

Sound: Call typically lasts from six to eight seconds. Begins as a soft buzz that grows into a penetrating rattle before trailing off at the end.

On the CD
One call each of two individuals

Range and Habitat: Found throughout most of eastern United States and
into southern Canada. Very common in the northeastern and northern
central states. Prefers deciduous forest. Often heard calling from trees in
city parks.

Sound: Call usually lasts eight to ten seconds. Starts off as a soft buzz that
increases in loudness and becomes a very rapid, high-pitched, pulsating
rattle before trailing off at the end. Sounds similar to the call of the
Swamp Cicada but is typically thinner and higher in pitch.

On the CD
Two typical calls of an individual

Range and Habitat: Found throughout eastern United States, but divided into various "broods" whose adults emerge synchronously every seventeen years, but on different years in different locations—in other words, this species can be found emerging somewhere over its range every year. Prefers deciduous forest, where it calls from the treetops.

Sound: Sounds quite unlike most other cicadas. Call is a harsh, low-pitched buzz lasting about two seconds and terminating with a down-slurred note: *zeeee-oh . . . zeeee-oh . . . zeeee-oh . . .* Emerge in great numbers to create a huge, clamoring chorus in the treetops.

On the CD
Closeup of individual (with Northern Cardinal), followed by large chorus

Master List of CD Contents

Species numbers throughout this book are equivalent to the track numbers on the compact disc. (The Linne's Cicada and Periodical Cicada share a track, since a CD can contain no more than ninety-nine tracks.)

MAMMALS

1. Eastern Chipmunk
2. Red Squirrel
3. Eastern Gray Squirrel
4. Eastern Fox Squirrel
5. Flying Squirrel
6. Woodchuck
7. American Beaver
8. Nutria
9. Meadow Vole
10. Common Muskrat
11. North American Porcupine
12. Gray Wolf
13. Coyote
14. Red Fox
15. Gray Fox
16. Black Bear
17. Northern Raccoon
18. Striped Skunk
19. Northern River Otter
20. Bobcat
21. White-tailed Deer
22. Moose

BIRDS

23. Barred Owl
24. Mourning Dove
25. Great Horned Owl
26. Eastern Screech-Owl
27. Whip-poor-will
28. Red-tailed Hawk
29. Red-shouldered Hawk
30. Broad-winged Hawk
31. Northern Flicker
32. Pileated Woodpecker
33. Red-bellied Woodpecker
34. Red-headed Woodpecker
35. Downy Woodpecker
36. American Robin
37. Northern Cardinal
38. Baltimore Oriole
39. Gray Catbird
40. Brown Thrasher
41. Northern Mockingbird
42. Black-capped Chickadee
43. Carolina Chickadee
44. Tufted Titmouse
45. White-breasted Nuthatch
46. House Wren
47. Carolina Wren
48. Blue Jay
49. Eastern Phoebe

50. Wood Thrush
51. Red-winged Blackbird
52. Common Yellowthroat
53. Eastern Towhee
54. American Goldfinch
55. Song Sparrow
56. Chipping Sparrow

REPTILES
57. American Alligator
58. Timber Rattlesnake

FROGS AND TOADS
59. Spring Peeper
60. Western Chorus Frog
61. Northern Cricket Frog
62. Gray Treefrog
63. Cope's Gray Treefrog
64. Green Treefrog
65. Green Frog
66. Bullfrog
67. Wood Frog
68. Pickerel Frog
69. Northern Leopard Frog
70. Southern Leopard Frog
71. American Toad
72. Fowler's Toad
73. Southern Toad
74. Eastern Narrowmouth Toad
75. Eastern Spadefoot

INSECTS
76. Northern Mole Cricket
77. Fall Field Cricket
78. Allard's Ground Cricket
79. Tinkling Ground Cricket
80. Carolina Ground Cricket
81. Striped Ground Cricket
82. Snowy Tree Cricket
83. Broad-winged Tree Cricket
84. Black-horned Tree Cricket
85. Common Meadow Katydid
86. Handsome Meadow Katydid
87. Sword-bearing Conehead
88. Nebraska Conehead
89. Slightly Musical Conehead
90. Round-tipped Conehead
91. Northern True Katydid
92. Rattler Round-winged Katydid
93. Oblong-winged Katydid
94. Greater Angle-wing
95. Lesser Angle-wing
96. Broad-winged Bush Katydid
97. Scissor-Grinder Cicada
98. Swamp Cicada
99a. Linne's Cicada
99b. Periodical Cicada